OCCASIONAL CONTRIBUTIONS FROM THE MUSEUM OF
ANTHROPOLOGY OF THE UNIVERSITY OF MICHIGAN
NO. 3

STANDARDS OF POTTERY DESCRIPTION

BY

BENJAMIN MARCH

WITH AN INTRODUCTORY ESSAY BY

CARL E. GUTHE

Ann Arbor
UNIVERSITY OF MICHIGAN MUSEUM OF ANTHROPOLOGY
Reprinted, 1967

© 1934 by the Regents of the University of Michigan
The Museum of Anthropology
All rights reserved

ISBN (print): 978-1-949098-60-0
ISBN (ebook): 978-1-951538-60-6

Browse all of our books at
sites.lsa.umich.edu/archaeology-books.

Order our books from the University of Michigan
Press at www.press.umich.edu.

For permissions, questions, or manuscript queries,
contact Museum publications by email at umma-pubs@umich.edu or visit the Museum website at
lsa.umich.edu/ummaa.

TABLE OF CONTENTS

	PAGE
A Method of Ceramic Description	1
I. Introduction	7
II. Body Description	11
III. Hardness	17
IV. Color	23
V. Surface Texture Glazed Wares	31
VI. Surface Texture Unglazed Wares	35
VII. Crackle	38
VIII. A Ceramic Pantograph	45
IX. Records	51

PLATES

PLATE		PAGE
I. Glaze Texture	*facing*	32
II. Unglazed Surface Texture	*facing*	33
III. Crackle		42
IV. Crackle		43

FIGURES IN THE TEXT

FIGURE		
1. Ceramic pantograph		46
2. Interchangeable pantograph points		47
3a and 3b. Basic curve and developed drawing		49
4. First record card		52
5. Second record card		53
6. Third record card		53
7. Fourth record card		54
8. Fifth record card		54

A METHOD OF CERAMIC DESCRIPTION[1]

CERAMIC specimens furnish important data for use in the detailed study of the archaeology of a restricted region as well as in the interpretation of the larger problems of diffusion of extinct culture traits. Yet little attention has been given to the special problems incident to the adequate description of these specimens. In order that publications on ceramics may prove of the greatest value, a form of description must be adopted which treats of all, and not merely of some of the characters of pottery, and which is, within the limits of the subject, comprehensible to investigators in related fields.

Since pottery making is a culture complex, the product is incapable of description by hard and fast rules, similar to those used by systematists in biology. It is possible, however, to formulate principles of treatment based upon the major characters of the material. Such a study is essentially an objective one, in which all the factors considered exist within the specimen itself, isolated from its cultural and environmental surroundings. The problem before us, then, is to present a broad, practical outline of the way in which a given specimen or group of specimens may be described in order to reproduce adequately a clear and definite mental image in the mind of the specialist. This problem has four distinct aspects, based upon the four primary characters of ceramic material, which are paste, surface finish, decoration, and form.

THE PASTE

There are four attributes of the paste or body which must be considered in rendering an adequate description.

[1] This is a revision of a paper which appeared originally in *Papers Mich. Acad. Sci., Arts and Letters,* VIII (1927), 23–29.

The most obvious of these is the composition, the clay proper and the non-plastic materials. In some instances chemical analyses are advisable. In those classes of pottery in which the non-plastic material can be differentiated from the clay by inspection alone, special attention should be given its degree of coarseness, and its relative quantity in proportion to the clay.

The second attribute of paste is its texture. The cross-section of a specimen discloses at once the degree of thoroughness with which the potter treated the paste before construction. In earthenware the paste usually has an irregular texture, which may vary in fineness within a single cross-section, or in different parts of the same specimen. In the technically more perfect examples a more uniform, finer texture exists.

The third attribute of the paste is its hardness, which depends only in part upon the degree of heat to which the specimen has been exposed in the kiln. A standard scale to which ceramic hardness can be referred is essential.

The fourth and most variable attribute is color. The composition of the paste determines the color in a general way, though the firing also has an effect upon it. In earthenware this attribute shows greater variation within a single specimen than in stoneware or porcelain. It is necessary to distinguish between the surface and the interior color of the paste, and between the color of the paste and that of various types of surface finish.

The Surface Finish

The term *surface finish* refers to that dominant feature of a ceramic specimen which is the result of a uniform treatment of the major part of its surface. It is the character upon which the first rough classification is usually made. Because of the interpretation frequently given the words *decoration* and *ornamentation* to include all embellishments of the paste itself, the real diagnostic value of the surface finish has not been appreciated. This second character is not the result of a step in construction but rather of a complex technique. The first stages of the treatment of the surface may occur before the specimen loses its plasticity, while the last stage may be the ultimate one in construction.

There are two major forms of surface finish. The first is the result of manipulation only of the surface of the paste, by processes known as smoothing, paddling, scraping, and polishing. The second is obtained by coating the paste with a variety of substances, such as clay slips, mineral washes, coats of tree-gums, wax, oil, and the like, or alkaline, salt, lead, or felspathic glazes. The latter may or may not conceal the effects of the former.

Except in the most simple wares, the surface finish is the result of a combination of treatments. Most surfaces which have been coated have first been smoothed or scraped. The coating, in turn, may consist of several layers, of different colors and materials. In describing the surface finish of a specimen which has been coated, four attributes should be mentioned: the substance used, the color, the texture, and the thickness of the coat.

The surface finish is also affected by a series of factors entirely distinct from those of construction. These are the result of the treatment after completion, in which use, time, or weather may cause the addition of material, discoloration, change in texture, flaking, or complete decomposition and disintegration.

Occasionally variations of surface finish, caused by inherent qualities of the methods or materials used, have a supplementary decorative value. Yet the study of the surface finish presents so many problems quite distinct from decoration, that it is advisable to treat it as a separate ceramic character.

The Decoration

The third of the ceramic characters is the decoration, the problems of which are of two kinds: those which deal with decorative design, and those which deal with decorative technique. An adequate study of design must be based upon an interpretative consideration of the elements and motifs, which are so varied that they constitute the special problem of investigators working in individual cultures.

The processes or techniques by which these designs may be applied to ceramic material fall naturally into two groups: First, that group in which minor alterations are made in the surface to be decorated, by use of a series of processes which result in incised, engraved, or pressed patterns; second, that in which the design is formed by adding material to the surface. There are four general processes in this group. The first, and most widely spread, is the application of paint. The second is the use of enamel, confined largely to glazed surfaces. The third is the addition of paste in small quantities to form a raised or applied pattern. The fourth is that of incrusting the surface with fragments of shell, wood, various metals, and similar materials. Of course, all of these processes may be further subdivided by recognition of refinements of technique.

The decoration of a specimen is usually the result of a combination of two or more of the processes mentioned. It may also be associated with the surface finish in a variety of ways. The design may occur over or under the various coatings. In fact, the decoration may be done at almost any stage in the construction.

The description of the design alone, while properly occupying the major part of a report on a special ceramic group, does not constitute an adequate discussion of the decoration. The various techniques used, their relationships to each other and to the surface finish, must also be fully described.

The Form

In form, the fourth and final ceramic character, the shapes encountered are myriad. It is possible, however, to indicate certain aspects of this character which should be treated in an adequate description. The first consideration is that of the methods by which forms are achieved. These are three, by use of the wheel, the use of moulds, and the dexterity of the potter's hand alone.

The following discussion applies to containers only, because they form the bulk of comparative material, and because an attempt to include all forms would confuse the issue. Emphasis must be placed on the importance of grouping material by criteria of shape alone. An attempt to use related and highly suggestive criteria, such as use, size, and functional additions, will cause confusion.

The accepted method of studying form is by means of cross-sections, but a single vertical cross-section through the center of the vessel is not always sufficient. The potential value of a series of sections should be considered with reference to each piece studied.

It is possible to subdivide the form for descriptive purposes into body shape, basal shape, oral shape, and the shape of the secondary features. Body shape refers to that part of the vessel upon which its fundamental shape depends. The basal and the oral shapes are those which result from specialized treatment of the lower part, and the mouth of the vessel, respectively. Secondary features are those which result from the application of sufficiently large amounts of paste or other materials to alter or hide the body shape in restricted areas of the surface.

If the study of this fourth ceramic character is undertaken with an appreciation of the essential individuality and the possible combinations of these four component parts of form, it is believed that the difficulties of classification by this character will be diminished.

Finally, the dimensions of a specimen should be included in a complete description. Measurements should be taken of the general size, and the cross-section of the body wall. The figures given should be the average of a series of measurements. In addition to greatest height and width of the vessel, it is often advisable to give the dimensions of each of the component parts of the form.

Wares and Styles

The use of the principles of description outlined in these pages will result in the grouping of materials according to various criteria under such terms as *wares, styles,* and *types*. At present these may have several meanings, some of which have the weight of general acceptance to their credit. Carefully worded, practical, and accurate definitions for each of them in publications will tend to correct the existing indiscriminate manner in which they are used. In the original text of this essay the following definitions were suggested.

"A ware is a ceramic group in which all attributes of the paste and the surface finish remain constant. A style of decoration is a ceramic group in which decorative design and technique both remain constant. A style of form is a ceramic group in which the form as a whole remains essentially constant, and is distinguished by some outstanding feature. A type is a ceramic group wherein the similarity is a generic one of all four characters caused by the entire pottery complex of the designated culture group."

This publication presents a general scheme of ceramic description which it is hoped may stimulate discussion and research in this rather neglected field, to the end that an improved methodology will increase the value of ceramics in the study of culture development.

C. E. G.

STANDARDS OF POTTERY DESCRIPTION

I

INTRODUCTION

How may the University of Michigan's Chinese celadons from the Philippines be compared with the fine examples of the ware that are preserved in the Freer Collection? This was one of the questions that faced me when I started to work under the provisions of the late Charles Lang Freer's bequest to the University for research in Oriental art. Ideally, perhaps, the pieces should be laid side by side, but as long as one group is in Ann Arbor and the other in Washington the practical difficulties are insuperable.

Lacking the possibility of direct examination of both collections at the same time, the necessity arises for a descriptive method sufficiently accurate and standardized to permit comparison on the basis of documentary records. The need for such a method has long been felt by ceramists, and many curious attributions have resulted from the lack of it, from the effort to establish the identity of an unknown piece on the authority of an imperfect description of a known piece. Loose use of terms has been so confusing as seriously to handicap comparative study, and a significant step was taken by the archaeologists working in Mesopotamia when, at a meeting held in Baghdad on 16 January 1930, they agreed upon a uniform nomenclature for describing in their reports the surface finish of pottery.[2]

[2] See a communication from the Abbé de Genouillac in *Syria*, XI (1930), 307–308. I am indebted to Dr. Neilson C. Debevoise for this information and reference.

In the biological sciences standards of description obtain, but the problem faced by the archaeologist is different in many respects. The naturalist deals with forms and substances governed by forces that tend to reasonable stability and more or less identical repetition. It is most unlikely that any flock of ducks will suddenly decide that wings would be more becoming if inverted in their attachments, and proceed to invert them. Once a species has been described, it is usually sufficient thereafter to identify the individual with the species and take his characteristics for granted, safely presuming that shape, coloration, structure, and other features will conform to the type.

The archaeologist, however, is dealing not with the accustomed habits of nature, but with the whims and vagaries of the human genius. What that genius will produce in the combination of natural materials, in the manipulation of structure and form, is subject to no law, or to so many that their interworking is scarcely predictable. A ceramic ware may be defined within close limits of color, texture, and body composition, but the shape and decoration of individual pieces will show remarkable variation. No single ware name will call up a precise and single picture to the mind, nor is it possible that it should so long as men remain creative.

Even though classification cannot be so precisely attained, and even though a description must be applied to each separate piece, it is quite possible to establish such standards as to make the descriptive process simple and uniform. It is possible to reduce color, surface texture, hardness, and other aspects to terms having a constant quality. They may not be absolute in denotation, but they can be so restricted that taken all together they will provide a sound basis for comparative study and identification.

In the comparing of pottery, indeed in comparative study in general, the important necessity is not so much absolute refinement of one criterion as the establishment of a sufficient number of criteria to provide a total view.

The same glaze color may suggest affinity between two specimens, but that single feature alone is not enough to determine kinship. All of the significant features of each piece must be related in terms of stable standards if an adequate conception of the likeness or difference of two pieces is to be formed.

In an effort to arrive at suitable standards for ceramic description, to provide a basis for comparative study of pottery from written records, the tests outlined in this report were developed. To attempt to set up standards and to claim for them universal adherence is a presumptuous undertaking. This much can be urged in favor of those here offered—that they have been demonstrated reasonable by actual use.

To be valuable, such standards require to be simple, and applicable without specialized knowledge beyond the normal range of the trained archaeologist or art museum curator. They should not involve the use of much, bulky, or expensive apparatus. They must submit the specimens to no special risks. The recorded results must be quickly intelligible. The extension of critical laboratory studies, in chemical and petrographic analysis, with the microscope and the x-ray, will augment our knowledge of ceramic structure and contribute to our information about the nature of various wares. Classification, however, must be in terms of those aspects of the material which can be immediately apprehended. The standards must be applicable to valuable whole and perfect specimens as well as to sherds. No effort is made herein to establish classifications, but rather to provide such descriptive foundations as will permit classification by workers in special fields in terms which are not only mutually equivalent among the students in that field, but also intelligible to specialists in other cultures.

With this pamphlet as a manual, the additional equipment to be employed consists of one book, a set of crystals, and a pocket flashlight, the whole costing not over seventeen dollars, and the bulk inconsiderable. The pantograph is an extra piece of laboratory equipment which is useful but not absolutely essential.

It is a matter for regret that systematic nomenclatures for describing shapes and decorative designs cannot be offered here. Both are needed, but an effort to provide them would unduly delay the circulation of standards that cannot be applied too soon if they are applicable at all. Probably no written description of form and decoration will ever take the place of a drawing or photograph of the object. Varying details of basal and oral construction, for instance, will always require illustration, but good photographs accompanied by descriptions based on the standards here proposed should make comparative study of pottery scientifically practicable.

II
BODY DESCRIPTION

The body is the structural element of pottery, and its most apparent attribute is shape. An acceptable effort to systematize the nomenclature of pottery shapes would be of great value, but it cannot be attempted here. At the present time there is considerable variation in the uses of descriptive names for various forms of pots. Common usage ascribes approximate connotations to such nouns as *vase*, *bowl*, *plate*, and the like, but they are inadequately delimited. The effort is not infrequently made by archaeologists to class pieces according to some functional grouping, so we have *food bowl* and *water jar*. The classical archaeologists have solved their problem so far as Greek pottery is concerned by the use of well established Greek names; and Dr. J. C. Ferguson has proposed that the Chinese names for porcelain vessels be adopted as descriptive standards by Western students of Chinese ceramics.[3] Individual attempts to develop systems of definition have been numerous, but no plan so far proposed has achieved general acceptance.

My present purpose is rather to discuss the description of the composition of the body, and this may very well begin with an examination of the term *pottery* itself.

We find the term used in two distinct senses, one with a formal implication and one referring to material. Thus, we speak of pottery, as distinguished from ceramic products used in building and in industrial processes, meaning chiefly vessels of domestic utility and decorative nature to-

---

[3] Dr. John C. Ferguson, "Shapes of Porcelain Vessels," *Journal of the North China Branch of the Royal Asiatic Society*, LIX (1928), 50–58, 15 plates.

gether with certain small objects of art. At the same time we use *pottery* to distinguish the less refined earthenware and stoneware from the superior porcelain, and speak, for instance, of Chinese *pottery and porcelain* to include the whole range of Chinese ceramic vessels and small decorative objects. Here, however, even though the primary implication is one of material difference, we are not free from the idea of form, for we seldom think of bricks and tiles and architectural ornaments as being made of pottery.

For purposes of consistency it would be advisable to restrict the scientific use of the word *pottery* to one of the two general meanings commonly given to it, preferably to its interpretation on a basis of form rather than of material.

The reasons for this preference are several and substantial. When we examine the whole field of ceramic production we find that it naturally divides itself into three main departments. Building materials, including brick and tile, architectural ornaments, and sanitary wares, form one obvious group. Crucibles, storage tanks insulators, and the myriad other ceramic objects used in industrial processes, in chemical laboratories, in power transmission, constitute another definite department. The third and most familiar group includes vessels for the domestic preparation and serving of food and drink, containers and storage jars, lamps and candlesticks, vessels primarily for ceremonial or ornamental purposes, and various bijoux. Under special circumstances ceramic sculpture might occupy a separate category, although most of the fired clay examples of the sculptor's art may conveniently be placed in the first or third of the departments outlined.

Again, the idea of form is never absent from the word *pottery* even when it is used with a primary material significance. The restriction of its meaning based on criteria of shape and function would therefore seem more logical than a limitation to description of the nature of the paste.

Finally, the limits of the word *pottery* when used with reference to the body material are not clearly defined, and there would seem to be no advantage to be gained from the use of the term in this connection when the various major types of body composition are already classified by such well understood nouns as *earthenware, stoneware,* and *porcelain.* When used to denote material *pottery* may mean everything that is not porcelain; or it may mean porous wares, approximately synonymous with earthenware; or it may imply wares that are not white in body, leaving quite undescribed several varieties of material.

We can speak of the first group as architectural, of the second as industrial, but there is no simple term other than *pottery* which is equipped by present connotations to stand for the third group.

Earthenware, stoneware, and porcelain represent the three major classes of body composition; as terms they are clearly defined, and their use, while making the employment of *pottery* as a material description unnecessary, at the same time gives that word a specific value when used with reference to form and function. Porcelain is characterized by its hardness, whiteness, and translucency. Stoneware is dense and vitrified, but lacks always the translucency and usually the whiteness of porcelain. Earthenware is porous in some degree, and the wide variety of products included in this class justifies the further distinction between coarse and fine earthenware.

As there is almost no limit to the variety of body composition that can be had from mixing different clays in varying proportions and by combining clay with other materials, numerous special names have been given to and accepted for particular wares. Thus we have hard and soft porcelain, calcareous earthenware, felspathic earthenware, bone china, proto-porcelain, and many others. As all of these have been competently discussed in A. B. Searle's *An Encyclopaedia of the Ceramic Industries*,[4] there is no point in attempting further definition here. It is strongly recommended that every serious student of ceramics acquaint himself with this work, and regard it as an authority.

It is, after all, the practical potter whose usages should be standards of technical description and discussion for the theoretical ceramist. Unfortunately, the archaeologist or art museum curator usually has little or no experience in ceramic practice and small acquaintance with the industry. This fact becomes obvious when we consider, for instance, the variance of intention in the use of the word *temper*. To the archaeologist, especially but not exclusively the American working with Indian pottery, temper is the non-plastic material added to clay, or occurring naturally with it, to reduce its stickiness and flexibility in construction, and its shrinkage and consequent danger of cracking in drying and firing. As a verb, *tempering* is the process of adding non-plastic materials, and the verbal adjective form is used in such phrases as *shell tempered* and *grit tempered*.

The practical potter, on the other hand, typically knows nothing of this use of the word. To him the process of tempering is that of moistening and mixing the various ingredients to a homogeneous paste of the proper consistency for the work in hand.

This latter use has the benefit of standing in both dictionaries and practice, while the former application is peculiar to American archaeology and to a few scholars influenced thereby. In such a sentence as: "In ancient pottery, the clay, well tempered with water, was almost invariably used without additional material,"[5] we find the term used consistently with ceramic practice.

---

[4] Alfred B. Searle, *An Encyclopaedia of the Ceramic Industries* . . . 3 vols. London: Ernest Benn, Ltd., 1929–30. In connection with the above, see especially I, 224; II, 434; and articles on various wares.

[5] *Encyclopaedia Britannica* (14th edition), XVIII, 339.

The adoption of the term *temper* as the name of a material or group of materials may have been due to a scholar's misunderstanding of the practical employment of the word, or to an extension of the definition: "a substance added to or mixed with something else to modify its properties," which is specifically applicable to sugar manufacturing and to certain metals, just as the verb meaning "to moisten to a proper consistency and stir thoroughly" is peculiarly associated with the ceramic industries.[6] In any case the confusion is to be regretted, for such differences tend to prevent an adequate sharing of experience between the potter and scholar, when each might learn from the other.

The archaeologist's use of *temper* indicates, however, a very real need for a short and simple term that will serve as a generic denominator for all non-plastic materials in pottery, and it may be worth while to examine possible substitutes.

Grog is sometimes used in this connection, but it properly applies to pre-fired materials, and its extension in meaning is probably due to the fact that the average potter does not commonly use such natural substances as sand and shell.

The Encyclopaedia of the Ceramic Industries refers to *non-plastic materials*, but that is too cumbersome a locution to take the place of *temper* in general archaeological description. Similarly, *non-plastic* used as a noun is not phonetically simple enough to be attractive.

The French *dégraissant*, implying a thinning or making leaner, is used by some European scholars writing in English, and it has the merit of avoiding confusion; but apart from the undesirability of borrowing a foreign word if a native word will serve, it does not lend itself to convenient manipulation as noun, adjective, verb, and verbal adjective, as an ideal term should.

[6] Both definitions from *Webster's New International Dictionary*.

A canvass of available words leads to the suggestion, as a possible general classifier and substitute for the noun *temper*, of the word *aplastic*. It stands as an adjective in the dictionaries, but a nominative extension is easy to make. The implication of its meaning is direct, and its use would avoid present confusion. It leaves the combinations *non-plastic* and *anti-plastic* free for those who wish to distinguish by their use between those aplastics that are permanently part of the paste and those organic compounds that burn out in the firing. Its lack of simple and convenient verbal forms seems its chief drawback.

The suggestion is made without pressing the recommendation. The purpose of the immediate discussion is to lament the existing confusion of nomenclature and to urge simplification by making the language of the scholar conform to and be consistent with the usages of the practical potter.

III
HARDNESS

The nature, indeed the very existence of pottery, is directly due to the capacity of one plastic material, clay, to become permanently hardened when sufficiently heated. The unique combination of qualities that makes it possible to shape an infinite variety of forms and preserve them by baking, constitutes clay one of the most valuable of all natural materials exploited by man.

The degree of hardness of ceramic products is by no means arbitrary. Pottery ranges from an earthenware so soft it can be scratched by a fingernail, to porcelain which is an exceptionally hard substance. The principal factor in determining the degree of induration of clay is the intensity of the heat applied to it. There is then a general correlation between firing temperature and hardness, low-fired wares being typically soft, high-fired wares typically hard. It has been suggested that a specific correlation might be worked out, by which the firing temperature could be deduced from the measured hardness of the product. Such a suggestion presumes, however, that the temperature is the sole determinant of hardness; but since the duration of firing and the composition of the paste are also conditioning factors, the preparation of any simple and practically useful table of the relation of heat to hardness is impossible.

For purposes of objective description of existing wares it is sufficient that we should be able to define hardness in terms of some applicable standard. There is no doubt as to the general meaning of hardness, but when the selection or devising of a standard of measurement is in question the variability of the concept is apparent. Thus the hardness of an object may be tested by its resistance to crushing, to indentation, to scratching or abrasion, or, as with the scleroscope for metals, by the rebound of a steel ball. The qualities measured by these various means are not at all the same, and the results are scarcely comparable.[7]

As there is a degree of correlation between softness and porosity, and between hardness and vitrification, it has been proposed that hardness might be calculated in terms of the rapidity of absorption of a drop of water, or the extent of visible spread of a drop in a given time. Such a test is difficult to control adequately in detailed gradations, it checks a quality related to hardness but which is not hardness, and it is liable to too great latitude of subjective interpretation.

It is a very common thing to see an archaeologist or connoisseur try a piece of pottery with a pocket knife or a fingernail to see whether or not he can scratch the body or glaze. This provides a rough and ready test by which ceramics may be grouped into three classes, the intermediate of which is highly variable. Thus, there are wares too hard to be scratched by a knife blade, of which porcelain is the chief, and at the other end of the scale is earthenware so soft that it can be abraded with a fingernail. Between these two is a considerable range of material which can be scratched with more or less ease by a good steel blade. Such a system of testing is hardly applicable for purposes of fairly exact definition.

The fact, though, that a simple scratching test is already commonly used suggests that a further development of such a test may be practical and acceptable. To be acceptable as a standard measure of hardness for our purposes, a system must have several essential qualities. It must be uniform, and objective; it must be simple and quick to employ; it

---

[7] For a more complete discussion of the several methods of testing hardness see Alfred B. Searle, *op. cit.*, II, 176-178.

must require no complicated, costly, or bulky apparatus; it should involve no computations; and it must submit the specimen to no risk of breakage or damage. The last condition is important because perfect pieces of great value must be described as well as sherds.

The one practical type of test which seems best to fulfill the requirements above outlined is an abrasion or scratching test employing a series of standard substances of known hardnesses. Such a test relates to the bond rather than to the whole mass of the paste, but except in the cruder forms of primitive pottery in which unfused aplastic is present in visible particles, this limitation has no practical importance. This one drawback is counterbalanced by the fact that resistance to abrasion is a more desirable practical quality in pottery than is resistance to either crushing or indentation.

The difficulty in trying to establish such a test lies in the problem of securing a suitable graded series of standards. The scale which has been used to some extent is that of Friedrich Mohs, which is the standard of mineralogical classification. In this system minerals are serialized in terms of their capacity to scratch and to be scratched by other minerals. Ten steps are established, from foliated talc to diamond, numbered 1 to 10. The minerals constituted as standards are tried *in order* against an unknown until two are found of which one will scratch and the other be scratched by the unknown. Then the hardness of the tested specimen is said to lie between that of the known pieces. Occasionally mutual abrasion will occur, when the hardness of the unknown is equal to that of the known.

The chief defect of the scale is that the gradations are relative. That is, the difference between 6 and 7 may be more or less than the difference between 4 and 5. Hardness 8 is not exactly twice as hard as 4, nor is 6 exactly half way between 4 and 8. A second difficulty is that the minerals themselves are not absolutely constant. In working out the scale, however, the steps were graded as fairly as possible with reference to reasonably uniform minerals.

For our purposes it is not as important that hardness be expressed in absolute terms as that the standards of reference by which descriptions are formulated be the same for all workers in the field. Availability of the standards, in terms of both distribution and cost, is an item to be weighed in this connection.

The minerals of Mohs' scale are available, and a series selected of minerals that are stable and show a minimum of variability, including both the steps and the half steps, would seem to offer the most practical basis for hardness determination.

It might be possible with rigidly controlled formulae and conditions of manufacture to make a series of ceramic standards for ceramic classification, but such a group would be subject to the same criticisms levelled against the mineralogical scale, and would have no distinct advantages sufficient to justify the experiment and expense.

With the assistance and advice of Professors Walter F. Hunt and Chester B. Slawson of the University, several tentative groups of minerals were made up and tried. On the basis of experiment with a wide variety of pottery specimens the practical usefulness of the test was confirmed, and the following series was selected for recommendation as a standard scale.

2	gypsum	5	apatite
2.5	cryolite	5.5	willemite
3	calcite	6	adularia
3.5	celestite	6.5	vesuvianite
4	fluorite	7	quartz
4.5	chabazite	9	corundum

The half steps are the best practical approximations, and the whole series has been demonstrated serviceable in use. The series is started at 2 for the reason that while much low-fired primitive pottery, for instance, is softer than 2.5, none has yet been found that could be scratched by gypsum. The constitution of porcelain, the hardest ceramic product, is such that it is no harder than quartz, so that material which will scratch quartz is suitable for an upper limit, to avoid too much wear on the quartz crystal in producing mutual abrasion with porcelain.

In order that the tests may be as nearly uniform as possible, it is desirable that the minerals be obtained from a constant source and selected for this purpose. To facilitate the obtaining of such crystals the coöperation of Ward's Natural Science Establishment in Rochester, New York, was enlisted, and in consultation with them special, simple, and inexpensive mountings were designed and three different crystal sets prepared, which they are now ready to make available. The mountings consist of short wooden rods into the ends of which the crystals are affixed with a sealing wax which holds them firmly but makes replacement easy. Each rod is stamped with the hardness number of the crystal. Six rods are fitted into a divided wood block which furnishes a secure protective case that is small and sturdy. The list of crystals and numeral equivalents appears on the outside of the case. The sets are known as the *Ceramic Hardness Standards of the University of Michigan Museum of Anthropology,* and are lettered A, B, and C. Set A consists of six crystals from 2 to 4.5 inclusive, Set B of six crystals from 5 to 7, plus 9. Set C consists of the twelve crystals, utilizing both ends of the rods as mountings.

Set A is adequate to meet the needs of archaeologists working in the American field, for extensive experiments in the Ceramic Repository in the Museum of Anthropology have revealed nothing harder than 4.5. The same set will serve the student of primitive pottery generally. Set B is adapted to specialized study of the harder wares. Set C includes the whole range and will be necessary for the general ceramist and for the study of certain cultures such as the Chinese whose pottery production is highly complex.[8]

With the softer wares one stroke of a crystal is often enough to produce a scratch. With the harder ones, however, it is often necessary to rub one against the other. This rubbing may be in short strokes and need not make a mark more than one-eighth of an inch long on the unglazed portion of a vessel. The amount of pressure need not, apparently, be constant, but a firm bite will get results quicker. With a firm hold on the crystal rod, as strong a pressure as is comfortable and safe to apply, and short rubbing strokes which are readily controlled, the desired result is quickly obtained, and the impression is so inconspicuous as not to be objectionable even for art museum specimens. One caution may be added, in order to avoid excessive wear on the softer crystals, tests should proceed from the harder toward the softer standards.

Already in the application of these tests body differences in visibly similar pieces from different times and sites have been demonstrated, and extensive use of hardness standards in description will undoubtedly add to our knowledge of historic and archaeological wares.

[8] *Ceramic Hardness Standards of the University of Michigan Museum of Anthropology* may be ordered from Ward's Natural Science Establishment, Inc., P.O. Box 24, Beechwood Station, Rochester, New York.

IV
COLOR

Of all the attributes of pottery none is more immediately impressive than color. While a connoisseur will assay the aesthetic merits of a vase primarily on the basis of its shape, the decorative value of ceramic vessels is generally conceived almost wholly in terms of color.

Color is a primary criterion for ready identification, and consequently it is the most available characteristic for general classification. Thus we speak of red ware and buff ware and black-on-white ware among the potteries of the American Indians, and of blue-and-white, celadon, and other wares among more highly advanced potters such as the Chinese.

It is especially unfortunate, then, that there is among students of ceramics no accepted standard of color nomenclature which would insure a positive and permanent interpretation for each color term used in the description of a piece of pottery. The problems involved scarcely require elaboration, but one or two examples may be cited by way of illustration.

In the study of Chinese blue-and-white wares we find that the general type is easily distinguishable, but that the dating of individual pieces is largely a color problem. The technique employed to produce this type of decoration was underglaze painting with cobalt, but since the quality of the cobalt employed varied from time to time the changes in color quality are the clues to period identification. Now it is said that the finest grade of the so-called *Muhammedan blue* once seen is impossible to forget, but this is more true as an aesthetic experience than as a sound basis for judgment. A study of a wide range of pieces will show that the differences between pieces may be relatively slight, although the total range of blue may be large, and except to one with very long experience or with a comparative series for matching ready at hand, exact recognition of the blue is extremely difficult. It is hardly a scientific approach to look at a piece and then at the reign mark and to guess that the color should be clearer or darker if the dating implied by the mark is to be accepted. An established series for comparison of the unknown against the known is not as commonly available as might be desired.

The man who is not a specialist in Chinese ceramics but who wants to be able to establish a reasonable bond of identity between a piece in his collection and a piece reported as standard from some other collection is in a particularly difficult situation, and even the expert cannot pretend to certainty in his understanding of the ordinary written description of a newly discovered or classified piece or ware.

The peculiar gray-green glazes known as celadons present complications that are similarly difficult. In China celadon glaze has been applied to porcelains and fine stonewares since the ninth century at least, reaching the peak so far as aesthetic quality is concerned probably in the thirteenth century. Distinctions have been drawn between the colors of several different kilns in the thirteenth century, and between Chinese, Japanese, Korean, and Siamese celadons, as well as between the celadons of different periods in China, but no description has yet proved really adequate. The Chinese have typically compared the celadon color to the tint of young onions, but they never mention how young the onions should be, and the color mutations through a few days of growth may be very noticeable. Grass is a very unstable basis for exact comparison, and when one observer calls celadons grass- or onion-green, and another refers to them as olive in hue it is apparent that confusion must arise.

Color plate reproductions of standard known pieces have a considerable value and are helpful to a degree, but they are not sufficiently accurate in the whole range of color rendering to furnish a true basis for precise comparison.

What is obviously needed in order to permit communication of sound and dependable information between students is a standard color nomenclature in which the content of color words may be exactly defined. This means, of course, that they must be referred to a standard method of insuring as far as possible that the same color sensations will be experienced by all the users of the words. It is probably theoretically impossible for two persons to have exactly the same color perception, but a reasonably objective method may be devised for providing the same opportunity for two persons to have the same color experience.

Analysis of color by means of the Maxwell disks or some other laboratory device, and description of the analysis in terms of a resultant formula should be accurate, but the method is rather too complicated to be generally applied.

It is apparent that what will be of the most practical value is a matching series of standard color samples that may be made available to all students. In order to be acceptable as a working standard the selection of samples must be well planned to present as complete a range as possible of effective variations, it must be produced by a process that will render all of the samples the same and permanent, and it must be so arranged as to be usable with a minimum of complication.

In the two decades since its publication in 1912, Robert Ridgway's *Color Standards and Color Nomenclature*[9] has been commonly accepted by zoologists and botanists as a standard reference. It contains samples of 1,115 named

[9] Robert Ridgway, *Color Standards and Color Nomenclature*, Washington, D.C., 1912, published by the author. Printed and distributed by A. Hoen & Co., Baltimore, Maryland. Pp. 44, 53 color plates.

colors, and until the last few years was the most usable matching series available. It has, however, certain serious handicaps, outstanding among which, from the ceramist's viewpoint, is the comparatively small range of specimen colors. Adequate description of the exact variations of clay, pigment, and glaze colors found in pottery requires a much more finely graded scale than is provided by Ridgway. A second unfavorable qualification is the uncertainty of a standard composed of pigments that have to be handled with great caution in respect to exposure to light. Further, the effort to provide names for the entire range of color samples resulted in some confusion in the use of adjectives.

Of more recent date and more valuable to us is *A Dictionary of Color* by A. Maerz, Director of the American Color Research Laboratory, and M. Rae Paul, Consulting Colorist of the Research Laboratories of the National Lead Company, published in 1930.[10] Technical advances in the preparation of pigments and inks have made possible reasonably permanent recording of 7,000 color samples, accurately graded and so conveniently arranged as to make reference easy.

As the book is opened to the color plates, the right hand page shows 144 samples (72 in a fourth of the pages) printed in twelve vertical files lettered A to L, and twelve horizontal ranks numbered 1 to 12. On the left hand page is a diagram ruled to correspond to the color plate. In spaces corresponding to the appropriate samples are such names as usage has rendered acceptable to define certain specific colors. Naturally a great many samples have no names, and the authors have made no effort to supply them, but reference is readily made by quoting plate, file, and rank. Scarlet, for instance, is 1 L 12. Incidentally, most of the names used by Ridgway are recorded against the samples

---

[10] A. Maerz and M. Rea Paul, *A Dictionary of Color*, New York: McGraw-Hill Book Company, Inc., 1930. Pp. 207, 56 color plates.

STANDARDS OF POTTERY DESCRIPTION

corresponding to his, so that transition is not difficult from the older system to the more comprehensive one.

The plates are arranged in seven groups of eight each, and each group comprises gradations of the ranges red to orange, orange to yellow, yellow to green, green to blue-green, blue-green to blue, blue to red, and purple to red respectively.

The work is easy to use, and full explanations accompany the plates in the text, which is itself a valuable document on color standardization. A north light is preferable for matching, but not absolutely essential in the case of pottery, provided an ample window is available and the match is not attempted in direct sunlight. The use of masks of light cards with holes the size of the color samples is desirable to isolate special areas in a polychrome piece and to avoid the influence of adjacent samples in the standard, but they are not necessary in matching the general color of a whole monochrome specimen. They may, in fact, even be misleading in such an instance.

In the case of polychrome wares, the individual specimen must determine the extent to which color description should be carried. Here a word of caution may be thrown in to warn against the unwisdom of overelaborating the detail of one's notes. The function of a practical description is to give as simply and concisely as possible that information about a specimen which will be of genuine value in comparative study. Undue and insignificant complication leads only to confusion, when clarity is essential. To attempt to set down every hue and nuance in a porcelain elaborately painted in overglaze enamels would be to waste time that might be better employed. The specialist who has handled many pieces of a ware will know that certain colors have significance and others none. To illustrate, the differences between Chinese *famille verte* and *famille rose* are not only conditioned by the amount of green but also, and chiefly, by the nature of the red or pink. Such determining colors should be specifically noted, but others need only be named in general terms. In case of any doubt it is probably better to err on the side of fullness of data, but experience will indicate just eliminations. The value of any system is that it saves time and effort, but it is not difficult to become enslaved to a too meticulous scheme and thereby lose all the benefit that should accrue from its employment.

When treating wares on which two or three different colored glazes are used, it would again be folly to attempt to record in detail all the gradations that may appear. Usually it is sufficient to note the typical aspect of each color, the aspect in which it appears at its highest value. Similarly in a flambé glaze it is only the significant hues that require to be definitely identified. Practice may well vary according to the character of the piece. Thus, it may be sufficient to define the prevailing color and remark the general nature of the variations, or it may be desirable to note the extremes between which variation occurs.

Primitive potteries often show a considerable color range as the result of irregular conditions of firing. Where a piece is all red, let us say, but has a large area of black on one side, the problem is not difficult. The uncertainty arises when one is asked to label a pot or a sherd in which gray, buff, brown, and red all occur in small areas imperceptibly blended the one into the other. If such a piece is held at arm's length or farther from the eye, the various colors will ordinarily blend to produce one prevailing impression, which may be identified and recorded. Where the range is too marked, as between black and buff in a single sherd, the major influences may be cited and the fact stated that one blends into the other. It is not infrequently desirable to make some comment on the relative areas of the different colors, as for instance: "$\frac{2}{3}$ yellow beige (13 H 7) blending through burnt umber (15 A 12) to $\frac{1}{4}$ black."

The technique of color matching is treated by the authors of the *Dictionary* on pages 11 to 13. There they note the difficulties encountered in comparing materials of different textures, and emphasize the necessity of keeping constant the angles of observation and of incidence of light. Occasionally, with pottery of a very rough texture, it may be desirable to throw the eyes slightly out of focus so that a blur of color impression will register rather than a sharp textural image. When identifying the general sensation of a whole sherd it is wise to place the sherd against a background of the same color as the mask used to isolate the color sample in the chart.

In recording the color data in notes it is advisable to give a color name for quick recognition, followed by the exact sample quotation in parenthesis. Thus, for example, we may describe a color as "apple green (18 J 6)," or, if it be not an exact match, "approximately apple green (18 J 7)." In each case the exact definition of the color recorded is given in terms of the plate, file, and rank of the matched standard. Familiarity with the *Dictionary* may serve to eliminate the descriptive words in the notes of some workers, but they should be included in published reports and descriptions for more immediate visualization by students less well acquainted with the standard.

In the study of celadons the general range of the term is fairly well understood, but we find a wide range of gray-green and blue-green tints included in the classification. The differentiation of Lung-ch'uan celadons in general from the specialized Chang yao, and both from the later products of Chingtechen will necessitate exact color definition of known or reasonably certain examples. As yet no adequate study has been made, but it is hoped that the extensive celadon collection of the Museum of Anthropology will yield some valuable information on type ranges and the relation of color to other attributes.

Certain examples of celadons may be cited from specimens in the Freer Gallery of Art in Washington, D. C., a collection noted for the superior quality of its contents. The standard celadon of Maerz and Paul is 21 B 4, in the yellow to green group. A bowl regarded as of Lung-ch'uan type but later than Sung (960-1280 A.C.) in the Freer collection has a glaze 21 B 5, almost the standard. A vase of what is generally known as Sung dynasty Lung-ch'uan type, however, has a glaze of 26 C 5, in the green to blue-green group. A small bowl described as "late Sung, Lung-ch'uan type" has a glaze of 28 D 5 approximating French gray. A Korean celadon bowl is glaze 30 A 3, in the green to blue-green group, and two bowls of Northern celadon type fall into the orange to yellow group, 14 I 2 and 14 J 3 approximating silver fern.

Here are data recorded months ago, and the memory of the exact colors of the various pieces examined at the time is too confused and uncertain for accurate matching, but with the Maerz and Paul *Dictionary* available, the colors of the Freer examples can always be compared with the colors of celadons in the Museum of Anthropology or elsewhere, and thus studies of the limits of variation of certain wares and other pertinent problems can be carried on with a measure of dependability impossible unless the data of various collections can be brought together and correlated by reference to common standards.

The *Dictionary of Color* has been tested with reference to potteries of many wares, to the pigments with which the Pueblo potters painted as well as to the Chinese glazes, to the clay as well as to the decoration, and each new test has but reaffirmed its right to be accepted as the color standard for ceramic description.

V
SURFACE TEXTURE

GLAZED WARES

The very term *glaze* implies and connotes a glossy or polished surface, but actually the variations in the surface quality range from a high degree of gloss to a dead matte. This variation may be produced in the manufacture of the glaze, or it may be the result of the disintegration that is sometimes incident to burial, exposure to certain acid conditions, or other more or less accidental circumstance.

Mutations in the gloss of the glazed surface take various forms. The most common, perhaps, is the minute pitting of the surface which produces the *eggshell* texture. In this case the glaze is usually glossy by nature, but the effect or appearance of polish is reduced by the lack of perfect smoothness over the surface.

The true matte glaze is usually of a crystalline structure with a prevailing dullness. An effect very similar is often produced in the disintegration that sometimes occurs during the burial period of archaeological specimens.

The degree of glossiness in the surface of pieces not exposed to the actions of external forces of disintegration depends upon the chemical constitution of the glaze, and upon the conditions of firing. Both of these are factors which may be expected to vary from kiln to kiln and ware to ware, and they may be expected to be constant within reasonable limits for kilns and wares. Thus, if a given period is noted for a ware of a certain color, a difference in surface texture is very likely to be a clue to the distinction between the authentic early production and a later but fairly successful imitation.

It does not always hold as an invariable determinant that the surface texture will vary from kiln to kiln, ware to ware, and time to time, but it is an additional criterion which is worth noting for its possible contribution to the solution of doubtful attributions. Its significance may not be constant, as is that, for instance, of color; it cannot of itself form a basis for classification; but in order to render an adequately complete description it is necessary to take cognizance of surface texture. Only upon descriptions that give attention to such details can be built up dependable classifications that are sufficiently solidly established to be adopted throughout the field.

The terms *gloss* and *matte* represent the degrees at and toward extremities of variation in glaze surface texture, and they have occasionally been qualified by such words as *high, semi-, dead.* If, however, the description is to be valuable it must be objective, that is, it must be referred to a common, acceptable, and available standard. It is necessary also that whatever test or measure is used should be simple and easily applied.

The most apparent characteristic of a glossy surface is probably its reflective quality, and it is not difficult for anyone to observe that the degree of sharpness of a reflected image diminishes as the surface becomes more dull and matte, until a surface entirely lacking in gloss reflects no image whatever. Whether it be the bars of a window or the filament of an electric lamp by the illumination from which a piece of glazed ware is being examined, the phenomenon is obvious.

In the Detroit Club glossimeter[11] the idea of reflected window bars is employed in a very practical device for measuring the gloss of paints and varnishes and flat surfaces generally.

---

[11] See Sophus Bolme, "Accurate Gloss Measurement by Practical Means," *Paint, Oil and Chemical Rev.*, XCIV (1932), 47ff.

PLATE I

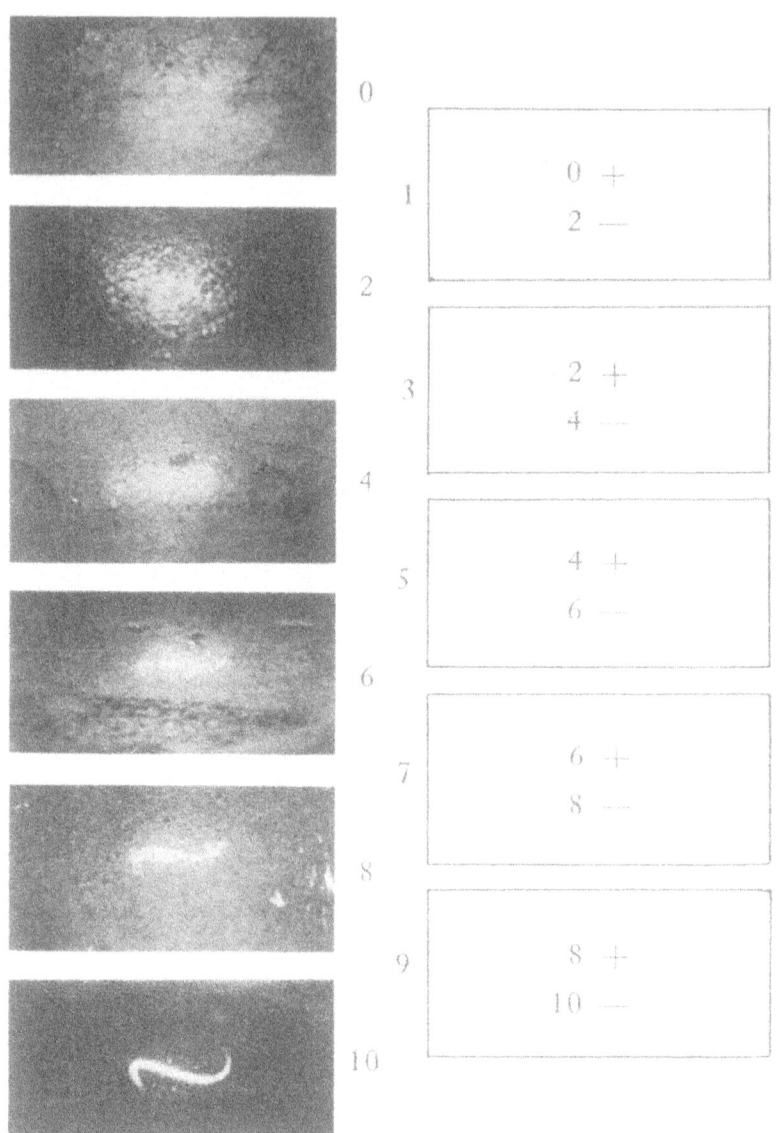

Glaze Texture

PLATE II

Rough

Smooth

Imperfectly
Polished

Highly
Polished

Unglazed Surface Texture

The method here proposed is based on the reflection of a light source, and, as it requires no apparatus beyond a pocket flashlight and is adaptable for use on curved as well as plane surfaces and in small areas, it is practical for ceramic description for the man in the field or in the laboratory. A student usually has to take his data where he can get it, and it is convenient if his measuring devices and references can be carried in a pocket or a briefcase to museums, private collections, or wherever he may have to work on material.

In the accompanying plate (Plate I) will be found a series of eleven areas graded from 0 to 10. In the even numbered spaces are six photographs of the reflection of the S-shaped filament of the lamp in a simple electric pocket torch without a lens. In measuring the gloss of a piece of pottery the pocket torch is held horizontally, and the surface to be checked is held at an angle of about 55° from the horizontal, almost in contact with the bulb of the torch. The reflection is then noted and graded by comparison with the standards in Plate I. When the reflection matches or approximates one of the standards the glaze is given the number of that standard. When it is definitely between two of them it is given the appropriate odd number. Thus a piece may be relatively described as matte, semi-matte, or glossy for purposes of ready description, and further set down numerically for accuracy. By reference to this scale texture 6, for instance, will be a quality constant within limits sufficiently close for practical purposes.

The scale was arrived at by making an extensive series of test photographs under standard conditions of pieces of different surface texture taken from the collections. In order to establish limits, a piece of polished plate glass was taken as 10, and a piece of smooth unglazed ware as 0. A Leica camera was used for the recording, set on a copying stand with the lens axis vertical and the film horizontal. A 2.2 volt bulb supplied from a battery was clamped in such a position that its axis was horizontal with the long center portion of the filament likewise horizontal. The pieces to be recorded were so set that a portion of the surface directly below the lens and almost in contact with the lamp maintained an angle of about 55° with the horizontal. It was found that a variation from 45° to 60° made no appreciable difference in the reflection. When the series of photographs was completed it was graded, and eleven samples that presented even steps from 0 to 10 were chosen. These were in turn employed practically for measuring different pottery fragments, and the sherds, arranged seriatim independent of reference to the standards, checked the photographic samples as correct. The series of eleven steps was simplified after further experiment to six as it now stands, and checked again by practical use with undescribed sherds. It has demonstrated itself as sufficiently accurate, elastic, and simple to warrant its acceptance as a standard.

It may be urged that this is a method for measuring only one feature of surface texture. It is true that there are certain phenomena such as crinkling due to irregular shrinkage in the glaze itself, irregularity due to underfiring, and the like, but even in those instances the scale is applicable, and the special condition is readily set down in a few words as one of conformation rather than texture.

In practice 10 is not to be found in ceramic glazes, although some pieces closely approach it. That is not surprising, however, when it is considered that there is an appreciable difference between ordinary window glass and polished plate. The lowest grade, 0, is seldom attained. Even the dullest glaze is likely to retain a capacity for a diffused sparkle or glitter to distinguish it from the softer glow reflected from unglazed wares.

So we have a scale for describing surface texture which has proved itself in use, and which provides a simple means for objectively establishing an additional attribute.

VI

SURFACE TEXTURE

UNGLAZED WARES

Having developed a satisfactory scale for the analysis of the surface texture of glazed wares, considerable effort was expended in the attempt to do something similar for unglazed wares. Several different types of tests were devised and tried, but none proved to have the desired practical applicability, and they were one by one discarded. The chief difficulty lay in the fact that the surface texture of unglazed pottery is conditioned by circumstances that lack the consistency inherent in the nature of glaze. Both the character of the paste and the technique of the potter contribute to determine the quality of surface texture. The degree or lack of levigation of the clay, and the introduction of various types of aplastic serve to modify the results a potter may obtain with his paste, and his methods of finishing his work are various. Ideally, surface texture should be isolated from surface treatment in description, it should be viewed as an objective and existing phenomenon and not from a methodological standpoint. Within limits this ideal may obtain, and the quality of body surface may be reported without reference to such manipulation as cord marking and paddling; however, the textural condition of the surface of unglazed wares is never independent of the actual touch of the potter's hand, and it is primarily this effect which makes the invention of a simple uniform scale seem impractical.

Curiously enough, while the actual variation of surface texture in unglazed wares exhibits a greater change than that observed in glazed wares, the necessity for fine differentiation is not so marked. Certain general and well marked types occur, and it appears possible to establish three principal groups with corresponding adjectives which will be sufficient to describe this single feature.

The first group may be called *rough*. In a strong cross light the shadows cast by surface irregularities are plainly noticeable. The finger run lightly over the body is sensitive to variations, and may even be impeded. Such a surface is most commonly due to the coarseness of the aplastic used in the paste, the particles of which are readily visible and tangible.

It may be objected that the adjective *rough* is capable of ambiguity, as it is used also to describe products of careless or unskilled craftsmanship. Such double use of certain words is perhaps unavoidable. Rough, however, is exactly applicable in the present need, and it is generally advisable to employ words as far as possible, rather than more abstract symbols, as they already have a descriptive significance to the reader. The use of *rough* to describe a quality resulting from inferior technique of forming or haste in manufacture may well be eschewed in favor of such a word as *rude*. Thus a rude pot is one rudely fashioned and a rough pot is one having a rough surface.

The second class, in contrast with the first, is *smooth*. It is the surface of a homogeneous paste, neither rough nor sleek to the touch. A finely levigated slip flowed on a pot and unburnished produces the characteristic surface. A pot that has been scraped but not polished may be either smooth or rough, depending on the nature of the paste and the kind and coarseness of aplastic.

The third group is that in which the surface has been burnished until it has assumed a degree of gloss, capable of reflecting a white high light, and is properly described as *polished*.

This class might be further subdivided according to the quality of the polishing. Some workers burnish their pots until the marks of the polisher are quite or practically eliminated in the general evenness of the surface. Others, however, are content with a hasty polishing that leaves definite tool traces. Were this merely an individual distinction it might be ignored, but it seems to be typical culturally. Therefore, we may speak of *high polish* on the finer and more meticulously finished examples, and of *imperfect polish* on the less expertly worked pieces.

While there is an intimation of technique in this last term, and so it may be objected that its implications are broader than a simple description of texture, which is all that is meant to be included in this category, the logical alternative following *rough* and *smooth* would be *glossy*. That word, however, generally suggests a higher reflective quality than is to be found in unglazed wares, and as we speak of the degree of gloss in a glaze, it would avoid confusion if we did not try to apply it also to unglazed wares. The use of *polished* is reasonable if we recognize the fact that whatever gloss may appear in the surface of unglazed pots is produced only by burnishing.

Description of the technique of surface finish is independent of the description of surface texture. A string-marked pot may be either rough or smooth, but not polished.

The accompanying plate (Plate II) presents enlarged photographs of surfaces taken to be typical of the classes here determined. Theoretically, and to some extent in practice, there is a more or less even gradation from very rough to highly polished pieces. In the actual classification, however, it will be found that there is a rather clear demarcation between the several types so that true doubtful or border cases are not so common that confusion is apt to arise. Where these do occur they must be treated as objectively as possible in the light of the intentions of the distinctions.

VII

CRACKLE

Crazing or crackle in the glaze is a common phenomenon which is variously appreciated. Technically, of course, it is to be regarded as an imperfection, depending as it does upon a lack of adjustment between the coefficient of expansion of the body and that of the glaze. Its typical appearance is during the process of cooling the kilns, but it may not develop for weeks, months, or years. Occasionally an accidental condition will craze what seems to be a well adjusted glaze, and apparently crazing has occurred after the burial of many excavated archaeological specimens.

The Chinese, however, as long ago as the Sung dynasty, turned this defect into a virtue and produced wares in which crackle was intentionally developed for its decorative value. To heighten the effect a black or brown stain was often imparted to the fissures. An extraordinary degree of control is shown by the presence of different crackle patterns adjacent to each other in regular zones or areas of the same piece. Even all-over crackles were common, and certain crackle effects were secured by cracks of two widths which absorbed different stains.

The means of producing different types of crackle are not of present concern. What is immediately important is to try to define and describe the known types that are commonly encountered.

The Chinese in their literature on ceramics have habitually noted the presence of crackle, and have described various patterns by such terms as *fish-roe, ice crackle, plum-blossom, crab's claw, hundred dangers,* and *hundred frag-*

ments. As the terms were not very consistently used it is difficult to interpret them specifically in relation to the descriptive system here to be proposed, but they at least convey some sort of a picture to the active imagination.

European students of Chinese porcelain have generally contented themselves with noting the existence of crackle and limiting the description to such adjectives as *bold, coarse,* and *fine*. A few have made conscious but unsystematic attempts to describe the crackle pattern, and some have borrowed the Chinese phrases.

To the potter any appearance of cracks in the glaze of a sound body is crazing. The name *crackle ware* has, however, been given to those ceramic products in which an intentional crazing is produced for its decorative effect. So there has been a tendency to limit the term *crackle* to deliberately produced cracking, or to cracking of a fairly regular all-over pattern, and to apply *crazing* to obviously accidental or irregular cracks. Thus the term *crazing* tended, especially in the vocabulary of the art historian, to have a more or less derogatory connotation, to imply technical defectiveness in the glaze, while *crackle* meant acceptable decoration. There is a certain value in such differentiation, but the distinction is not always readily perceptible, particularly in archaeological specimens. The terms in their general use among potters, students of ceramics, and archaeologists are rather loosely interchangeable, and to attempt an arbitrary restriction would lead to needless confusion. It is easier, and probably wiser, therefore, to accept *crackle* and *crazing* as synonymous for practical purposes of description.

The linear patterns produced by crazing are infinitely varied, and a complete description of a crackle should take no less than eight criteria into account. On the basis of extensive examination of examples available in the Museum collections, these criteria have been summarized in the following table.

A. PRIMARY CRACKS
   1. No long continuous cracks
   2. A few long continuous cracks
   3. Pattern dominated by long continuous cracks
      a. Long cracks vertical or radial
      b. Long cracks horizontal or circumferential
      c. Long cracks spiral or irregular
B. SIZE
   1. Average width of areas or distance between cracks .125 cm.
   2. Average width of areas or distance between cracks .250 cm.
   3. Average width of areas or distance between cracks .500 cm.
   4. Average width of areas or distance between cracks 1.00 cm.
C. AREAS INCLOSED
   1. Fairly regular in size and shape
   2. Very different in size and shape
D. CRACK ENDINGS
   1. All cracks ending in other cracks
   2. A considerable proportion of cracks ending in space
E. QUALITY OF FRACTURE
   1. Cracks smooth and direct, as in glass or ice
   2. Cracks ragged, as the edges of broken earthenware
F. WIDTH OF CRACKS
   1. Approximately equal
   2. Noticeably different (especially apparent in two-color staining)
G. STAINING
   1. Unstained
   2. Even monochrome stain
   3. Two or more colors (including part unstained and part stained)
H. DISTRIBUTION
   1. All over
      a. Single type
      b. Two or more types
   2. Only in part
      a. Single type
      b. Two or more types

It is readily apparent that a formula could be developed from this analysis, with the addition of a few adjectives to describe color or the location on a vessel of different types of crackle, that would give a reasonably exact definition of any crazed condition. The value of a complicated set of symbols for one detail of ceramic description is questionable from a practical standpoint, however, and a simpler method should be devised if possible.

On examination of various specimens it appears that whatever the detailed variations of pattern may be, four

STANDARDS OF POTTERY DESCRIPTION 41

general type classes will prove adequate for all ordinary description. These may be called *open, crystalline, semi-crystalline,* and *amorphous,* and may be defined as follows:

OPEN crackle (or crazing): crazing in which a considerable proportion of the cracks or fissures end in space rather than in other cracks. This type might also be called suspended or incomplete crackle, for the tendency is for the fractures to develop until they terminate in other fractures. The condition is unstable, and extension of the crazing is provoked with relative ease by shock, temperature changes, or the normal processes of time. As distinguished from open crackle the three following classes may be described as closed or complete, as all or practically all of the cracks have reached terminals, and the condition is approximately stable.

CRYSTALLINE crackle (or crazing): crazing in which the pattern is dominated by long continuous lines of cleavage, typically approximately parallel, with the areas thus bounded divided and subdivided with moderate regularity as to size and shape. This is the most common of all types of crackle and is the only type which is readily found in all sizes.

SEMI-CRYSTALLINE crackle (or crazing): crazing in which the long continuous lines are either entirely lacking or are few, irregular, and not dominant in the pattern, but in which there is a definite division and subdivision of areas, usually very irregular in size and shape.

AMORPHOUS crackle (or crazing): crazing in which there are no long continuous cracks, and without any apparent subdivision of areas. The areas are usually more nearly uniform in size and shape than are those of crystalline crackle, and the cracks are not infrequently ragged rather than smooth.

Observation similarly shows that average measurements of the width of inclosed areas, or the distances between cracks, tend to fall into four general groups which may be defined as follows:

MINUTE: crazing in which the average width of inclosed areas, or distance between lines is approximately .125 cm., or less.

PLATE III

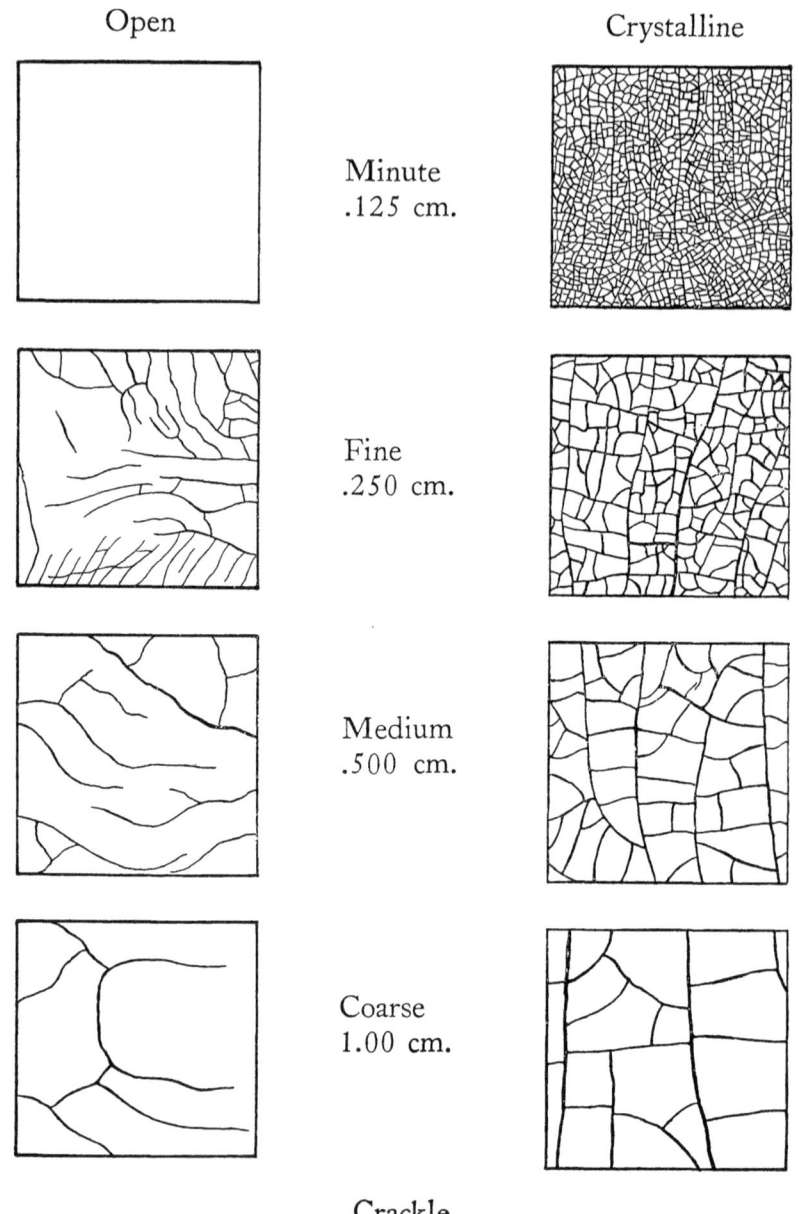

Crackle

PLATE IV

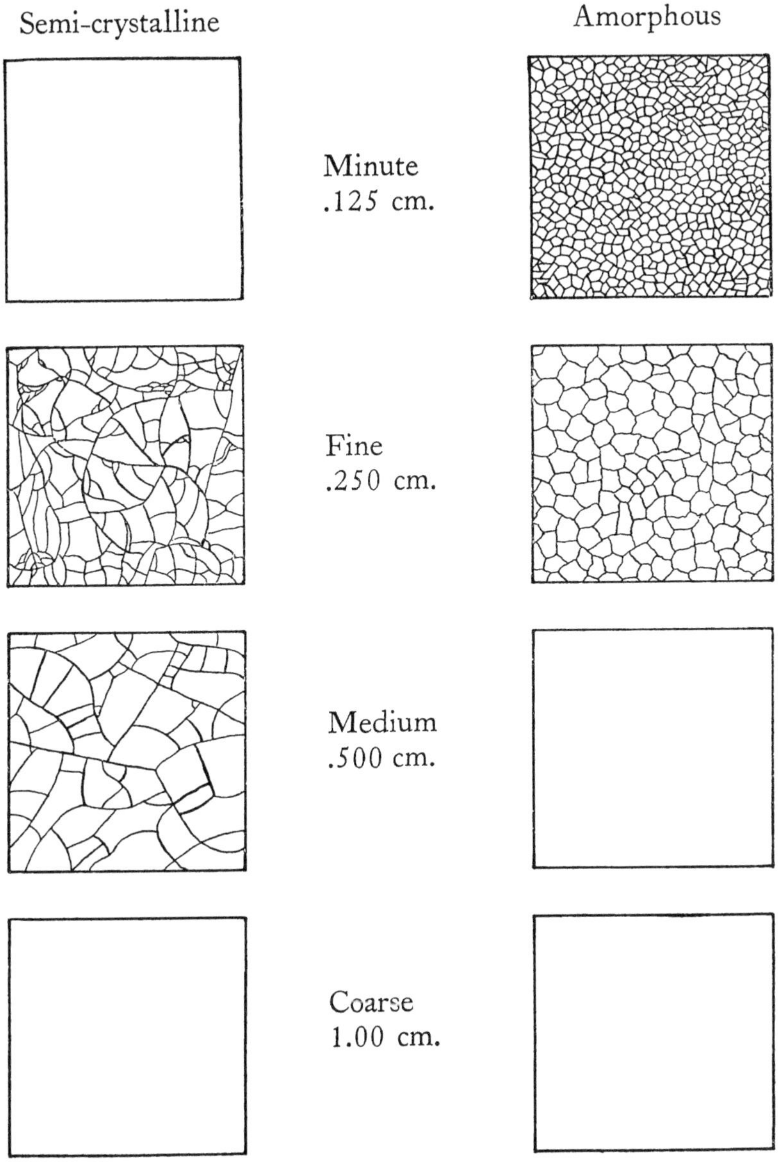

Semi-crystalline		Amorphous
	Minute .125 cm.	
	Fine .250 cm.	
	Medium .500 cm.	
	Coarse 1.00 cm.	

Crackle

FINE: crazing in which the average width of inclosed areas, or distance between lines is approximately .250 cm.

MEDIUM: crazing in which the average width of areas or distance between lines is approximately .500 cm.

COARSE: crazing in which the average width of inclosed areas or distance between lines is approximately 1.00 cm., or more.

In theory at least the four types of crackle pattern should be divisible into these four size categories, but practically the occurrence of certain types in certain sizes is either rare or unknown, so that in the preparation of the accompanying charts (Plates III, IV), which were drawn from actual specimens, five spaces of the possible sixteen could not be filled with available specimens.

The charts are reproduced to exact size, so that the matter of description may be further simplified by using them as comparative scales. The pattern classification is made more obvious by them, and an approximate matching of a given specimen as to size would serve for practical description to eliminate the laborious process of taking a series of measurements and averaging them.

Taking these two classifications of pattern and size as a basis, a satisfactory description can be quickly arrived at and easily set down. The term *medium crystalline*, for example, conveys an immediate impression, and supplemented by notes as to distribution, staining, and other distinguishing details is sufficiently complete.

VIII
A CERAMIC PANTOGRAPH

The essential importance of section drawings in comprehensive ceramic description is hardly to be questioned, but extensive use of such graphic data has been rendered difficult in the past by the relatively slow and laborious process of making them. With a view to eliminating the tedious labor of establishing the basic profile of a specimen by the usual system of measuring up and pointing over, Dr. Guthe conceived the idea of a device based on the principle of the common pantograph. With two minds applied to the task, tentative plans were drawn up, and the Engineering Shops of the University constructed two experimental models. They differed only in size, and the smaller one was installed in my laboratory in the Asiatic division of the Detroit Institute of Arts. As that one has been subjected to a variety of tests and has proved adequate for the ordinary needs of a museum laboratory it is described in detail here. The same results may be obtained with the larger machine, but it is more difficult to find space for in a workroom, and it is heavier and somewhat awkward to use on the pieces of moderate or small size that usually constitute the major share of a ceramic collection. For practical work it seems advisable to use the smaller machine on the majority of specimens and to draw very large vessels by the older method.

The ceramic pantograph consists of a long base board on which are mounted a divided platform with clamps for the object to be drawn, a vertical drawing board, and a pantograph set to operate vertically and produce an outline to a scale one half of that of the original object. (See Fig. 1).

While it would be possible to construct the pantograph with a variable scale it was felt that whatever gain there might be would be almost entirely theoretical, as for comparative study an arbitrary and established scale is most desirable.

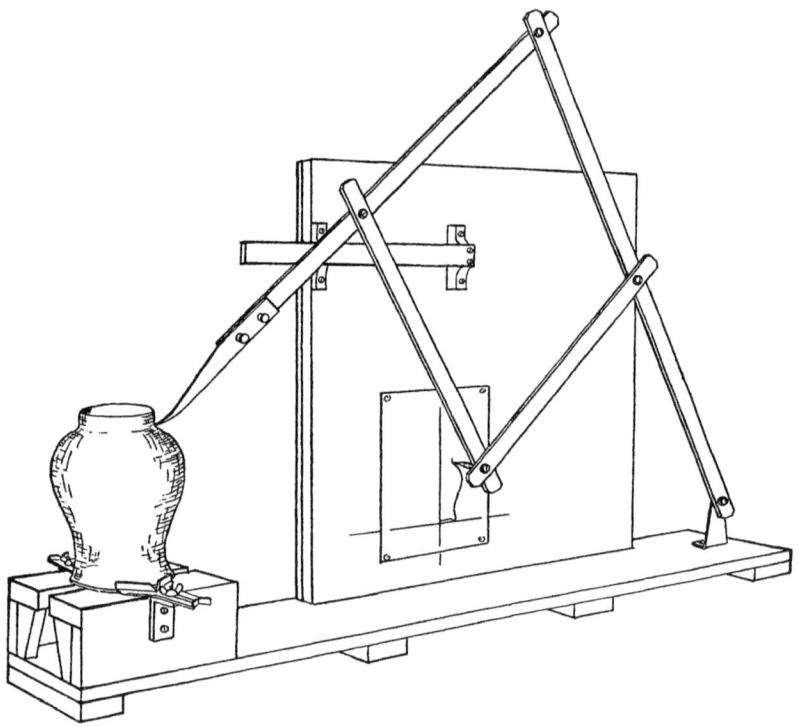

FIG. 1.—Ceramic pantograph.

The most significant feature of the device is the system of interchangeable points by which it is possible to draw up under the foot of a specimen or down inside the neck for an appreciable distance. Four points as shown in Figure 2 have proved a sufficiently flexible assortment for all average work on vases, pots, jars, bowls, and plates.

The machine here described works most effectively for objects not exceeding 18 inches in height and 24 inches in diameter. The base, object-platform, and drawing board are made of white pine, the pantograph arms of maple. The base is 54 inches long and 9 inches wide. The object-platform is 9 inches square and 4 inches high, divided in the middle to allow the points to reach up under the foot of the object. The table is provided with two aluminum clamps with flanged jaws open to a right angle. The jaws at the two ends

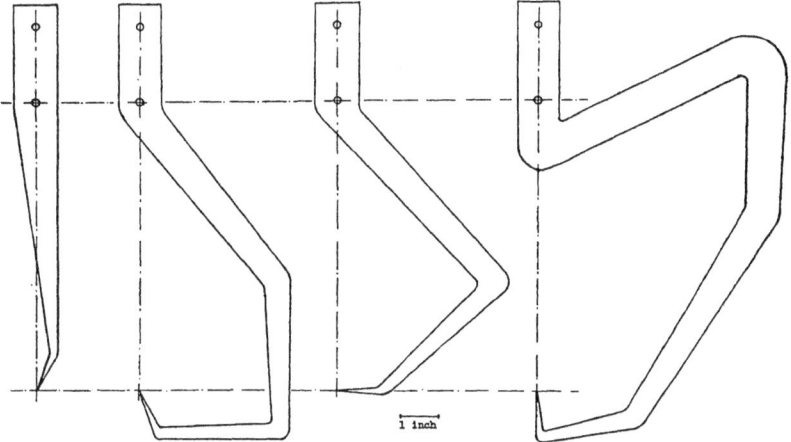

FIG. 2.—Interchangeable pantograph points.

of the clamps are reversible, one pair being half the size of the other with correspondingly lower flanges, so that objects of different sizes may conveniently be accommodated. The clearance from the center line of the clamps to the edge of the drawing board is about 14 inches.

The pantograph has two long arms with working length of 36 inches and two short arms with working length of 18 inches. For the scale adopted the short arms are fastened precisely in the center of the long arms. One end of one long arm is pivoted above the base board at the exact height of the object-platform, the free end of the other arm has two brass screws with knurled nuts to hold the interchangeable points. These points are cut of sheet aluminum one-eighth of an inch in thickness. The design of the points can be varied according to the need of the user of the apparatus, provided only that the contact-point be exactly centered with the arm from which it extends and so adjusted that it is equidistant with the pivot of the other long arm from the bolt that connects the two. Thus the points are made interchangeable, and it is possible by using several of them to get the complete outline of the specimen, including the foot and the rim. For facility in changing the points a spring letter clip may be employed in lieu of the nuts to hold the extension firmly on the bolts, which are, of course, fixed in the arm. The clearance between the contact-point of the recurved points and the end of the wooden arm is $5\frac{1}{2}$ inches.

The pencil holder, which, in common with all the fittings except the clamps and points, is of brass, is made to take a short section of an ordinary wooden pencil.

The pantograph, the open division of the object-platform, and the center of the object to be drawn are all in the same vertical plane. The drawing board, which is 27 inches square, is set back according to the length of the pencil holder, and a horizontal bar is fastened out from the top of the board to steady the pantograph arms. A horizontal line at the height of the object-platform, and a vertical line corresponding to its center are marked on the board.

The manipulation is simple. The specimen is centered on the object-platform and clamped in place. Two base lines are ruled on the drawing board corresponding to the top and center of the object-platform. It is convenient to use letter-size metric-ruled paper, to mark in pencil on the paper the base and center lines for the drawing, and to tack up the paper so that the lines on it match those on the board. If the pencil is well adjusted all attention may be given to following the contact-point on the specimen, but it is usually preferable to use the left hand on the contact-point and the right on the pencil. The outer surface is traced first, then the points are changed to get inside the rim and foot. The resulting drawing is a basic curve, mechanically accurate and true to scale, such as is seen in Figure 3a. To finish the drawing the curve of the other side of the specimen is completed with dividers, and the section with the use of calipers. If the specimen is not symmetrical, it may be turned around and

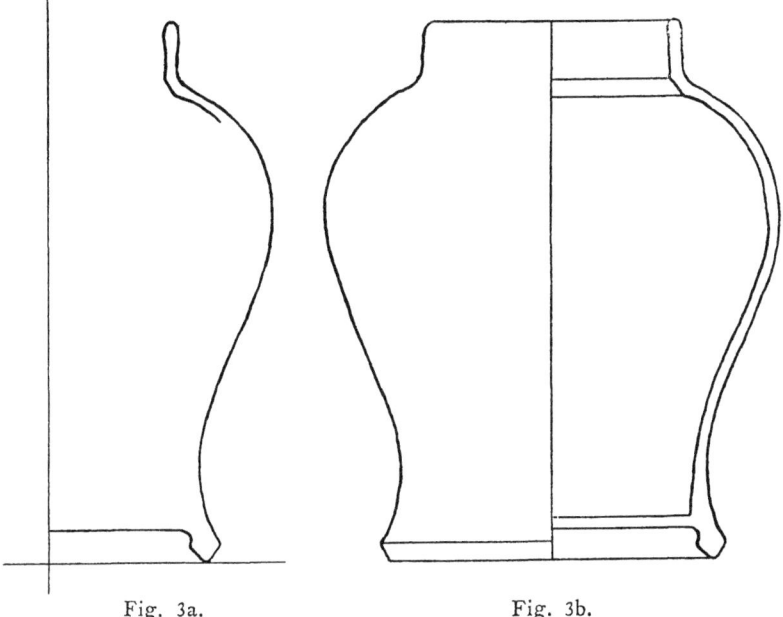

Fig. 3a.   Fig. 3b.

FIGS. 3a and 3b.—Basic curve and developed drawing.

a second curve drawn, and reversed with the dividers. A developed drawing, the left half external and right in section, is shown in Figure 3b.

As the pantograph was devised to gain speed and accuracy in making notes, it seems a useless procedure to take the trouble to ink the drawings after completing them. The work may be developed entirely in pencil and then sprayed with a fixative if it is to be much handled. A very thin solution of white shellac in alcohol is good, or a commercial fixative may be purchased. This has the effect of coating the drawing so that it will not rub. For reproduction an ink tracing may be made, the original may be on plain white paper and inked, or a paper ruled in very faint blue lines, which can be eliminated by the engraver through his photographic process, may be employed.

The making of the initial profile need not occupy more than five minutes, and the accuracy of it is mechanically assured. The development of the finished drawing will depend upon the amount of detail to be included. The making of sections by the pantograph has been found to be not only much quicker but also much easier than by the older method, and the machine has been used successfully with bronze vessels and for obtaining picture-frame profiles as well as for ceramics.

The construction of the apparatus is simple enough if precision is observed in joining the pantograph with reference to the center lines of the arms and the spacing of the bolts, and in the adjustment of the points so that the various contact-points bear an identical relation to the arms. While the apparatus is successfully workable, improvements are possible, therefore this publication is offered without detailed working drawings in the hope that the device will be developed and prove widely useful to other workers.

IX

RECORDS

Every individual worker will have his own method of keeping his records. Some there be who are wedded to their special systems beyond any hope of divorce or separation, while others will enslave themselves to new plans whenever such are offered. Without making any special recommendation in the matter, a method is herewith presented which has justified itself in practice and which may be of value to others.

Lightweight, 4 by 6 inch white cards are used, for several reasons. They are uniform with my general notes and other records, both personal and official. They are of a size large enough to write on comfortably, and small enough to carry in a pocket. They can be easily spread out for working, and compactly disposed of when it is time to drop them into their standard file, and they are large enough so that photographs and other material can be filed along with them, avoiding to a great extent the separation of the records about single specimens or subjects.

A set of five cards is used, with information forms multigraphed on them. The forms are complete enough so that if they are filled out with any degree of care no essential item of information will be missing. Supplementary information can be added on other cards, and small photographs may be mounted on standard cards, or a 5 by 7 picture can usually be advantageously trimmed to fit the file directly.

For ready filing a manila paper pocket is used for each set of cards pertaining to one object. These pockets are about 3½ by 5 inches in measurement, so that titles on the tops or ends of the cards are readily visible, and the cards can be quickly removed. They are folded and pasted in such a way that the right end and bottom are closed and the left end and top are open. They occupy very little space in the files, they serve to keep together all the cards pertaining to

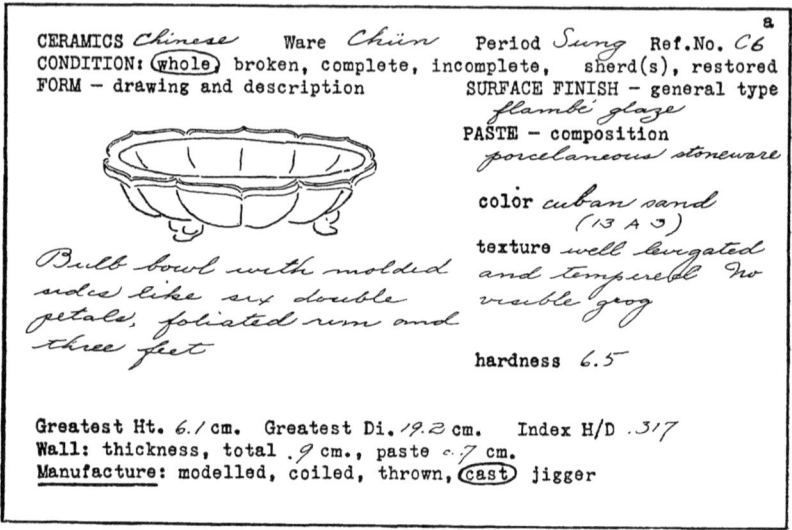

Fig. 4.—First record card.

one object or subject, and there is enough friction to bind the cards rather firmly in place and prevent the scattering that may occur when ordinary folders are used. Such pockets can be made to order, or they can be readily produced by cutting down cheap envelopes to the desired size. Even used manila envelopes that have come in through the mail have been made to serve.

While there is no urging here to use this particular system of cards, it is believed that the information required by the printed form is essential for a comprehensive permanent record of a piece of pottery. Certain items will naturally not be necessary in reporting some restricted cultures, but in a

STANDARDS OF POTTERY DESCRIPTION 53

```
CERAMICS  Chinese                              Ref.No. C6
FORM - details    Form and measurements    Surface finish
Basal  Flat base with three         Completely glazed,
cloud-scroll feet. Within           except ground feet
feet a ring of spur marks           glaze thinner than
       Bottoms of feet ground       on rest of body
off                                 Olive (15 H 7)


Oral  Rim extended horizontally     Glazed, olive
 in six ∩-shaped lobes              on edges and
with narrow raised edge             blue (36 B7) on
                                    surface inside
                                    edge

Secondary features
```

Fig. 5.—Second record card.

```
CERAMICS  Chinese                              Ref.No. C6
SURFACE FINISH          Outside          Inside
Uncoated
    manipulation

Slip - material
    color
    how applied

Glaze - composition
    color  olive (15 H 7) with blue (36 B7)   Olive and blue in
           and red (54 J 5) flashes            depressions and
    texture  olive transparent, red and       mottled over bottom.
             blue semi-opaque. Faint earthworm marks. Visible bubbles
    crackle  a few random cracks

    thickness c. 1 cm.  distribution  all over
Later changes - from use

    from time, weather, etc.
```

Fig. 6.—Third record card.

```
                                                                    d
CERAMICS    Chinese                                  Ref.No. C6
DECORATION              Outside                      Inside
Technique
                        None.


Design
```

FIG. 7.—Fourth record card.

```
                                                                    e
CERAMICS    Chinese                                  Ref.No. C6
HISTORY - Mark                     Present collection  Freer
  Numeral K inscribed              Cat. no.  gallery of art
  on base under glaze                        11.334
                                   negatives  Freer   H170 B2
                                              F.175

Provenance
    Purchased of _____     1911




Date examined
   14 VII 32
```

FIG. 8.—Fifth record card.

museum of anthropology where comparative study is to be made of various pieces, and where uniformity of record keeping simplifies study of the data, such a complete form is highly desirable. Then, too, if the outline is fairly complete one does not have the painful experience of wanting to use the records apart from the piece and finding that there has been neglect in noting some significant item of information.

A sample set of cards is reproduced herewith, and a careful examination of them will supply all the suggestion that could be given in a fairly lengthy essay. The space on the first card is sufficient for either a small drawing or a miniature photograph, and I have found the Leica a very useful instrument for making catalogue records. No amount of description will ever take the place of a pictorial representation for final identification and study.